Jack Nicholson

The Illustrated Biography

By Bill Hewitt
AND THE EDITORS OF LIFE

LIFE ICONS
Managing Editor Robert Sullivan
Director of Photography
Barbara Baker Burrows
Deputy Picture Editor
Christina Lieberman
Copy Editors Barbara Gogan, Parlan McGaw
Photo Associate Sarah Cates
Special Contributing Writer Bill Hewitt

Editorial Director Stephen Koepp

Editorial Operations
Richard K. Prue (Director), Brian Fellows (Manager),
Richard Shaffer (Production), Keith Aurelio, Charlotte Coco,
Tracey Eure, Kevin Hart, Mert Kerimoglu, Rosalie Khan,
Patricia Koh, Marco Lau, Brian Mai, Po Fung Ng,
Rudi Papiri, Robert Pizarro, Barry Pribula, Clara Renauro,
Katy Saunders, Hia Tan, Vaune Trachtman

TIME HOME ENTERTAINMENT
Publisher Jim Childs
Vice President, Brand & Digital Strategy
Steven Sandonato
Executive Director, Marketing Services Carol Pittard
Executive Director, Retail & Special Sales Tom Mifsud
Executive Publishing Director Joy Butts
Director, Bookazine Development & Marketing
Laura Adam
Finance Director Glenn Buonocore
Associate Publishing Director Megan Pearlman
Associate General Counsel Helen Wan
Assistant Director, Special Sales Ilene Schreider
Senior Book Production Manager Susan Chodakiewicz
Design & Prepress Manager Anne-Michelle Gallero
Brand Manager Roshni Patel
Associate Prepress Manager Alex Voznesenskiy

Special thanks: Katherine Barnet, Jeremy Biloon, Rose
Cirrincione, Jacqueline Fitzgerald, Christine Font, Jenna
Goldberg, Hillary Hirsch, David Kahn, Amy Mangus, Kimberly
Marshall, Nina Mistry, Dave Rozzelle, Ricardo Santiago,
Adriana Tierno, Vanessa Wu

Copyright © 2013 Time Home Entertainment Inc.

Published by LIFE BOOKS, an imprint of
Time Home Entertainment Inc.
135 West 50th Street
New York, New York 10020

ISBN 10: 1-61893-066-4
ISBN 13: 978-1-61893-066-8
Library of Congress Control Number: 2013938645

"LIFE" is a registered trademark of Time Inc.

We welcome your comments and suggestions about LIFE
Books. Please write to us at:
LIFE Books
Attention: Book Editors
PO Box 11016
Des Moines, IA 50336-1016

If you would like to order any of our hardcover Collector's
Edition books, please call us at 1-800-327-6388. (Monday
through Friday, 7:00 a.m.–8:00 p.m. or Saturday, 7:00 a.m.–
6:00 p.m. Central Time).

PHOTOGRAPHY CREDITS
Page 1: Jack, as Jack Torrance, brandishing the key to the
infamous Room 237 in *The Shining*. Tony Costa
Pages 2-3: Jack examining a set of still photographs,
at home, in 1969. Arthur Schatz
These Pages: Jack, with Dennis Hopper (left) and Peter Fonda
in *Easy Rider* (1969). Silver Screen Collection/Getty

Produced in association with
KENSINGTON MEDIA GROUP
Editorial Director Morin Bishop
Designer Barbara Chilenskas
Copy Editor Lee Fjordbotten
Fact Checker Ward Calhoun

Now, You Know Jack

HOLLYWOOD HAS HAD its share of stars. After all, there is something about the gigantic screens—and they are bigger than ever these days—that tends to elevate the actors to larger-than-life status from the get-go. This has produced a passel of matinee idols through the years, many of whom captured the public's attention for a nanosecond in cultural time, only to burn out and disappear as quickly as they emerged. In the rare air far above these pretenders are the genuine, enduring legends, the true icons, whose names remain etched in the memories of moviegoers for generations: Gable, Tracy, Bogie, Brando, De Niro, Pacino, Streep. In this book, we present one of the very brightest of those shining stars, a man we think we know so intimately that, in his case, the identifier is just a first name, and a common one at that: Jack.

The face, that marvelous plastic face, comes to mind first: the grin that speaks of devilish and frequently illicit pleasures, those arching eyebrows like twin suspension bridges floating above irresistibly mischievous eyes, that sensuous mouth, capable of spewing seduction and sass and sincere sentiment in equal measure. We think we know him, don't we? He's Jack, our Jack—would anyone refer to him as Nicholson? He's that guy we know from his performances: intense, like Jack Torrance in *The Shining* or the Joker in *Batman*; rebellious, like McMurphy in *One Flew Over the Cuckoo's Nest*; a smartass, like Jake Gittes in *Chinatown*; a tough, testosterone-driven man's man, like Colonel Nathan Jessep in *A Few Good Men*. These performances, marvelous all, are of a piece; they solidify our perception of the man, a perception further bolstered by the fun-loving rogue we see on parade at the Oscars, or courtside at the Lakers games, or bouncing in or out of some glittering Hollywood party. Jack the seducer, Jack the party animal, Jack the lover of intoxicants.

But what do we really know? As wonderfully chronicled by veteran magazine writer Bill Hewitt in the pages that follow, much of that public persona is indeed based on fact: Jack has been with an astonishing (exhausting?) number of women, he has openly taken a variety of drugs—he deserves a plaque in the marijuana users' Hall of Fame—and he has often lived his life as if there really were no tomorrow. But Hewitt takes us much deeper, back to Jack's birth in mysterious circumstances in New Jersey—Jack never knew for sure who his father was, and his mother's identity was kept from him until he was well into adulthood—back to his days as a struggling actor when Hollywood stardom seemed increasingly implausible, back to the insecurities that, yes, plagued his relationships with women. Round and round.

The triumphs are here: the sudden stardom after *Easy Rider* in 1969, the amazing run of brilliant movies and stunningly vivid performances that followed, the 12 Academy Award nominations, the recognition, the celebrity, the enormous amounts of money (Jack was ever a savvy negotiator). But in the end, what emerges from Hewitt's incisive profile, as well as from the terrific photographs—several of them from the LIFE archives, which first appeared in our pages—is the private Jack as well as the public persona: a man who does indeed revel in his image, who trades on it, who burnishes it with terrific exuberance at every turn, but who is far more complex, far more serious about his craft as an actor, far less confident in his relationships, far more concerned about his role as a father, particularly as he gets older, than the almost cartoon perception of Jack might suggest.

We promise: None of this will detract one iota from your enjoyment of the public Jack, the movie star Jack, the bon vivant, the electric personality with the megawatt grin. He is still playing that role, and playing it better than anyone who has ever lived. Lest you doubt this, jump on your laptop, go to YouTube and search for Jack Nicholson and Jennifer Lawrence. The clip you find will reveal a still irresistible Jack, at 75, interrupting Lawrence's interview with George Stephanopoulos after her Oscar win this past February and reducing the 22-year-old actress to a giggling school girl, beyond flattered to have met and shared a moment of flirtation with the great Jack. That Jack is in these pages too, in plenty of pictures.

How many Jacks are there? Why waste time counting? Enjoy them all, in these pages.

CHAPTER ONE

Jersey Boy

Mystery did not mar Jack's early days down the shore, where he spent a generally secure childhood growing into the Jack we'd come to know and love

IT COULD be said that the first chapter of his life was prosaic. It could also be said that it was operatic. Here was a kid who grew up in Jersey and didn't know who was who, no matter what he might have assumed. He let the people raise him who were raising him. He didn't really care, and these kinds of things happened during the Great Depression in places like New Jersey—and everywhere else. In the opera, much would be made of where-is-the-mom and who-was-the-dad, and everyone would be singing loudly. But in real life it was more a question of when's breakfast, and when's dinner.

He emerged. Well, he didn't really emerge, in any dramatic sense, but he went on, and caught on, and then proved himself. How much of his upbringing informed his later self can be speculated, but perhaps will never be accurately known; Jack Nicholson has, in his adulthood, always been willing to pose but not particularly willing to divulge. That is, certainly, his or anyone's prerogative.

But anyway: He came out of New Jersey as a different cat, to use a phrase of which he might approve, and he remained a different cat. His friend Robin Williams put the matter squarely, nodding certainly to Dean Martin's famous quote about Frank Sinatra: "There's Jack, and then there's the rest of us." For once in the Hollywood sphere, that wasn't idle flattery.

We know him because he is an actor, and in this, too—as much as Jack as a celebrity or Jack as a character—he has been nothing if not singular. For more than a half century he has been burning through the silver screen, inhabiting a cast of characters that stick indelibly in the mind. Nominated for twelve Academy Awards and the

In spite of the mysterious circumstances of his birth— not to mention the alcoholism in his family—Jack has always described his childhood as essentially happy.

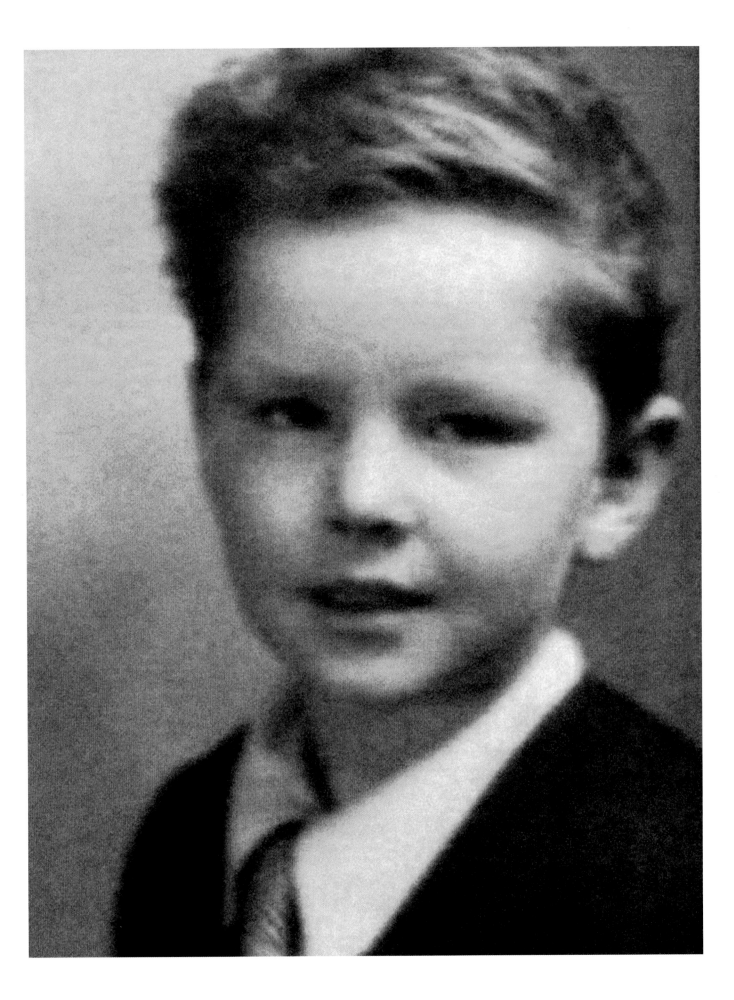

Jack's grandmother, known to everyone as Mud, was a devout Catholic, who feared the negative light that would be cast on her daughter June as well as on Jack (far right, after his first communion at St. Elizabeth's Church in Avon-by-the-Sea) should the truth of his birth become known.

winner of three, he is the one of the most decorated film stars of all time. There are names in Hollywood that belong to "immortals"—Garbo, Bogart, Brando—and one day, maybe tomorrow, there will be Nicholson.

What has been his secret, beyond the manifest talent? What has set him apart and above?

Physically, his smile gets most of the attention. That and perhaps those dancing eyebrows. But it's the eyes themselves that are his most arresting feature. You might say they were bedroom eyes—if the boudoir in question belonged to the Marquis de Sade. There's an intelligence and a knowing quality there. They can sparkle merrily and then go dead with menace an instant later; they are mesmerizing. You never know what's coming, but you can't wait to see what it will be.

You look at the long-ago photographs from the New Jersey boyhood and realize the eyes, and a lot of the danger, were already at play. Nicholson's introduction to the world of acting was haphazard and appropriately bizarre. He was born on April 22, 1937, in Neptune, a solidly middle-class seaside community. His father, John J. Nicholson, did window dressing and sign painting from time to time. His mom, Ethel May, known as "Mud" (for "Mudder" or mother), was a hairdresser who ran her successful business out of the family home. There were two older sisters, June, 17 years his senior, who wasn't around much, and Lorraine, 15 years older, who played a key role in raising Jack. Four years after John Jr. was born, John Sr. moved out of the home, returning occasionally in the years to come.

Even with the age differences and his father's relative distance, an observer might have said in the 1930s: Nothing so remarkable about any of that. Lots of families have lots of issues.

Except the whole thing was an elaborately-staged sham, right down to the date and place

Though only a junior, then-gentlemanly Jack accompanied Nancy Smith to her senior prom in 1953 after her date dumped her just before the big event.

Among the many titles bestowed on Jack in high school was "Class Clown"—no surprise there, though his brand of humor would become a bit more sophisticated in future years. Here he poses with his female counterpart, Sandra Sala.

of Jack's birth. Young Jack knew nothing about the details.

To this day, there's a good deal of mystery surrounding Jack Nicholson's early years. One thing is clear: The two people he regarded as his parents, John J. and Ethel May, were in reality his grandparents. And his sister June? She was his mother.

What in the world had happened?

Well, the teenaged June had been a fairly talented tap dancer. "June had it all: looks, brains and talent," June's sister, Lorraine, once told *Vanity Fair*. "She came home every day after school, pulled out the tap board we kept in the kitchen, and practiced. That was her life." Steely determination might have been one admirable trait June would pass on to her son.

After leaving school at 16, June began performing all over—the Northeast mostly, but

Jack discovered acting in high school, appearing in a minor role as a junior and then as the headliner as a senior (above, upper right, with the rest of the cast, including a clearly less-than-human baby).

also places as far-flung as Florida and Texas. Her career was under the supervision of one Eddie King, a well-known impresario in the New York City sphere. Not unnaturally, June had dreams of stardom. But then, as sometimes happens, romance intervened. She began keeping company with a young man named Don Rose, who was himself a singer and dancer performing along the Jersey shore. Nearly 10 years

older than June, Rose was also married, though he and his wife were separated. In the summer of 1936, he and June had a blissful time together, as can happen at the shore. And, as also sometimes happens, by autumn, bliss had turned into a baby—as they said back then, "in the oven."

When June informed Don that she was expecting, he immediately announced that he would marry her, never mind that he was already fully booked when it came to spousal gigs. For her part, Ethel May, the grandma-to-be, a practicing Catholic, was none too pleased with this turn of events. As she saw it, the arrival of a baby, whose father was already married, would do her daughter no good. She insisted that June go away to have the child.

According to family lore, John J. Nicholson Jr. was born at home in Neptune. Evidence suggests, however, that the real birthplace was a charity hospital in New York City. As for the exact date, it's a guess at best, since no birth certificate has ever turned up. (Later, his family managed to sneak him into public school without ever producing one.)

When June returned home, the charade was on, and then it was full-blown. The weirdness had other dimensions going forward. John J. Sr. was, for instance, a serious alcoholic. Jack later told an interviewer for *Playboy* that as a youngster he often went bar-hopping with Senior. "He was an incredible drinker," the actor recalled. "I used to go to bars with him as a child and I would drink 18 sarsaparillas while he'd have 35 shots of Three Star Hennessey. But I never heard him raise his voice; I never saw anybody be angry with him, not even my mother. He was just a quiet, melancholy, tragic figure—a very soft man."

And yet: For all this 20th century Dickensian melodrama, Nicholson remembers childhood as being pretty happy and (gracious!) normal. Ethel May was a hard-working woman who, when Jack was high school age, was able to move the family to tonier Spring Lake. "People can't believe I'm not upset by the deception, but how can I be upset by something that worked?" Nicholson told *Vanity Fair* in 1994. "These women were never anything but great with me, and I'm not being sentimental. If I never embarrass their spirit, I did good."

It would eventuate that more than a few people had their suspicions about Jack's true parentage. Some of the neighbors, for instance, whispered to each other that June was the real mother. As for the identity of the father, even within the Nicholson family there was a lingering question about Don Rose's role. Lorraine says that June and Mud were the only ones who knew for sure. A daughter of Eddie King, with whom June spent a great deal of time, came forward much later to claim that her dad was in fact Jack's father. Be all that as it may, and if you can't keep the characters straight without a scorecard, it doesn't really matter, because Jack himself says he never suspected anything until he learned the truth at the age of 36.

That in itself is a tale. In 1974, just as Nicholson was hitting it really big with *Chinatown*, a reporter for *Time* magazine was working on a cover story about him. In double checking the biographical details, a researcher began to sense that things were not adding up. Finally the reporter was able to piece together the truth. When the findings were presented to Nicholson, the actor was shocked, so much so that he asked the magazine not to disclose the facts.

Nicholson has said subsequently that, having become aware, he made no attempt to nail down the identity of his father. "I'm not overly curious," he insisted at one point. "I've always said that I had the most fortunate rearing. No one would have had the courage to design it that way, but it was ideal. No repression from a male father figure, no Oedipal competition."

(There is one curious upshot of all this: Jack, politically a staunch liberal, has long been an opponent of abortion, believing—no doubt accurately—that if the procedure had been legal and readily available at the time of June's pregnancy, he himself never would have been born.)

Jack was a bright kid who did well in school when he felt like it (he even skipped a grade). He loved drawing and the movies. *Thunderhead*, the sequel to *My Friend Flicka*, was a particular favorite: "My mom kept a box of pennies and I used to reach in there and take a handful and

Although not a star athlete or enormously popular with the girls, Jack (as framed in his high school yearbook) was admired enough for his wit and sense of humor to be voted vice president of the senior class.

JACK NICHOLSO
Vice-President

we went every day. That picture got me." He also showed early signs of the charm and sly humor that were to be his calling cards. He had a literary bent. "I was always a fantasist," he once told *The New York Times*. "I always wrote my way out of trouble in school. I had to stay after class every day my sophomore year, and they would assign you to write a 1,000-word essay story, and I'd write thousands of words. By the time I knew no one would be reading, I'd slip in all sorts of mean comments about the people who ran the school." Though younger than his classmates, he was popular and fit in well. "His smile was terrific," recalls high school chum George Anderson. "He made plenty of friends who spanned several classes. Jack wasn't one of the heroes, but he made them his friends."

By high school he had already acquired his lifelong love of sports. He dreamed of playing on the basketball team, but was too short and pudgy to make the varsity. He wrote about sports for the school paper instead, participated in school plays, and during horse racing season spent many a day at Monmouth Park Racetrack. "I

was a good handicapper. That's where I got my spending money."

Meanwhile, as Jack was making his way through high school, "sister" June had gone off and gotten married, living for a while in Detroit. She gave birth to two more kids, then got a divorce and headed out to Los Angeles, where she got a job as a secretary. She offered Jack an invitation to come out for a visit before he started college. (He had been considering the University of Delaware.) He took her up on the offer and crashed in June's tiny apartment in Inglewood in September 1954.

Accidentally, fatefully—as with everything else that had happened so far—Jack had wound up in Hollywood.

THE JACK NICHOLSON
THEATRE

COURTESY OF LEE WEISERT/MANASQUAN HIGH SCHOOL (4)

High School Confidential   Jack's senior yearbook contains a treasure trove of trivia about his high school career. (Manasquan High is shown opposite, below.) From his official entry (opposite, top) we discover that he was the manager of the basketball team—to his dismay he was never good enough to play—as well as a member of the Rules Club (Really? Jack?), the Study Club and the Table Tennis Club. The yearbook also reveals Jack's first in a long line of eccentric roles—the school would eventually rename its theater (above) in honor of its most famous graduate—that would extend across a 50-year career, as Hannibal (top) in *The Curious Savage* by John Patrick, which takes place in a mental institution where Jack's character is one of the inmates who compulsively plays the same two notes on his ever-present violin over and over and over. Shades of *One Flew Over the Cuckoo's Nest*? How about the obsessed Jack Torrance in *The Shining*?

JOSEPH NICHOLS

"Dutch"...a clown but real great...would be lost without lunch periods...a real asset to our basketball team.

Football 1, 2; Basketball 1, 2, 3, 4; Baseball 1, 2, 3, 4.

JOHN NICHOLSON

"Nick"...jolly and good natured...enthusiastic writer of those English compositions...his participation added to our plays.

Blue and Gray 1, 2, 4; Rules Club President 1, 2; Football 1; Basketball Manager 2; Study Club 3; Junior Play 3; Table Tennis Club 3; Senior Play 4; Class Vice-President 4.

GEORGE NOLAN

CHAPTER TWO

Paying Dues

*No overnight success, Jack spent
more than a decade in Hollywood learning
the movie business from the ground up*

AT MANASQUAN HIGH, which he attended while living in the apartment in Spring Lake, New Jersey, Jack had been voted "Class Clown" by his friends in the class of 1954. Makes sense. We cannot assess the competition all these years later, but it still makes sense. And although he spent the better part of an entire school year in detention, he is remembered as having been good in the parts he played on the high school stage. All of this seems to make sense, too: the detention, the theatricality.

Of course, these adolescent distinctions in New Jersey in no way could have armed him sufficiently for Hollywood. But if he had no prospects, he soon had a bit of a plan: show biz. That bare outline had served scores of others well in La La Land, so why not Jack?

Day to day, life was not easy. He and June didn't get along too well, what with the small apartment and her two young kids (Jack's half siblings, let's not forget), on top of June's no doubt complicated feelings about having her abandoned son underfoot as a daily reminder of a past she had probably been doing her best to forget. Jack was away from the apartment as often as he could be. He worked in a toy store for a while to make money. Finally he landed a job as a gofer at MGM. Movie-industry-wise, it was the absolute bottom of the ladder—the pay was $30 a week—but it was a foot in the door. His duties included biking all over the sprawling MGM lot to deliver the mail, as well as even more menial duties in the office.

By then, Jack had moved out of June's place and found his own apartment a few blocks from MGM. His roommate was Roger Anderson, who also worked at the studio. (It's worth mentioning at precisely this point: Throughout his life Jack has stayed in touch with friends he met along the way, whether they be high school chums or pals like Anderson who never quite made it in Hollywood. On his arm at his 50th high school reunion back in Jersey was his aunt, Lorraine.)

Jack adored the whole movie mishigas, and he and Anderson enjoyed hanging around the sound stages in their free time. He admired many of the leading men of the day, including James Dean and Henry Fonda, but his special idol was the magnetic Marlon Brando. He never could have presumed to dream at the time that, by a happy coincidence, once he had made it, and made Hollywood his home, he would be living a stone's throw from Brando's pad on Mulholland Drive.

Unlike other hopefuls at MGM, the young Nicholson seemed strangely ambivalent about pushing his own career. Then one day, the big break that every studio gofer dreams of landed right in his lap—and he brushed it off.

Stepping into an elevator, Jack crossed paths with producer Joe Pasternak, whose credits included *Destry Rides Again*. Pasternak noticed the young fellow, who incidentally had slimmed down considerably since his New Jersey days, and asked the million dollar question: Ever think about acting?

There is, of course, only one answer, but somehow Jack flubbed his lines. He shrugged, coughed and answered, "No." In his biography of Nicholson, *Five Easy Decades*, author Dennis McDougal recounts the hilarious exchange that

Jack (in costume for *The Raven* in 1963) found Hollywood a difficult place to break into in the early years, and he spent his twenties trying to find his niche, shifting back and forth from writing to acting—he even did a little directing and film editing. He would be 32 before the world would discover just how charismatic he could be onscreen.

ensued shortly afterward between Jack and his boss in the animation department, Bill Hanna (who would go on to become the first half of the genius Hanna-Barbera cartoon team, responsible for *The Flintstones* and so much else):

"Did Joe Pasternak ask you if you want to be an actor?" Hanna demanded.

"Yeah," said Jack.

"Well, what did you say?"

"No."

"Jack, let me ask you a question: Do you want to be a goddamn office boy all your life?"

Jack took the hint. He got himself a screen test, which went well. The one sticking point seemed to be his slightly honking New Jersey accent, a vestige of his time in the Garden State that he had not shed. He signed on for his first acting classes with a character actor named Joe Flynn, who eventually would find fame, of an undeniable sort, on television as Capt. Binghamton in the hit series *McHale's Navy*. One of Flynn's first pieces of advice, garnered from years of knocking around Hollywood, was to skip any voice lessons to "repair" Jack's accent. The wise Flynn told him, in effect: There are a million guys around here with silken voices. The goal is to stand out.

It was a lesson that Jack clearly never forgot.

From then on, he followed a fairly familiar (if lengthy) path to stardom. More acting lessons, this time with noted teachers Jeff Corey and Martin Landau (yes, that Martin Landau). He was awarded a spot in a local repertory company, the West Hollywood Players Ring, where one of his classmates was the young Michael Landon. Some TV work started to trickle in for him, including recurring stints on *Divorce Court*. The extra cash was a godsend, especially after Jack and all the other animation employees were laid off from MGM because the studio wanted to get out of the cartoon business.

Like many great actors, and perhaps more than most, Jack seems onscreen like a natural, someone who probably doesn't have to sweat it, and probably didn't have to strain to develop his talent. This is far from true, he's quick to insist. "Once I got started acting I loved it," he said in an interview. "I wanted to be the best actor possible. I work very hard at the craft of it. I went to classes for twelve years. There's nobody successful who didn't study a lot. It doesn't exist."

So he was working, but life, too, was progressing. June, the "sister" who was the actual mother, died of cervical cancer in 1963 at the age of 44. Ethel May, the "mother" who was the grandmother, died in January, 1970, of a muscular disease. "I felt that during her lifetime, I had communicated my love very directly to my mother," he said later. "We had many arguments, like everyone does with any parent, but I felt definitely that I had been understood. There were no hidden grievances between us. I had always fulfilled whatever her expectations of me were, as she had mine of her. I didn't feel any sense of 'Oh, I wish I had done this or that' at the moment of bereavement. I felt as good as you could feel about the death of anyone."

Back at the shop, Jack's apprenticeship dragged on for some 14 years. His first movie role came in 1958, when he got the lead, no less, in a cheapo thriller titled *The Cry Baby Killer*, the saga of a teenage holdup man. The

Among the many forgettable movies Nicholson appeared in for producer Roger Corman was *The Wild Ride* (1960), in which he plays a drag racer caught in a triangle of sorts with his best friend and his girlfriend (played by Georgianna Carter, his real-life love interest at the time). The script and the resulting production were mediocre at best—Corman paid his actors and writers next to nothing, hired novices to direct his movies and generally tried to restrict his budgets to a shoestring—but that didn't prevent Nicholson from continuing to hone his craft.

film may not have been a *succès d'estime*, but it was a success de box office, making a tidy profit. The architect of the whole thing was a young producer and director by the name of Roger Corman, regarded now as one of the great schlock visionaries in Hollywood history. He was to have a profound influence on Jack's career. Together they made six movies, with titles such as *The Raven* and *The Terror* and *The Trip* (not the family vacation kind, you should know). Among them was also one that would become a cult classic, *Little Shop of Horrors*, shot in two days, in which Jack played a screwball dental patient. Even in the bad stuff, he stood out, shining amid the dross.

Given the seriousness with which Jack approached acting, you might think he would look back on this phase of his career and wince. In fact, to this day he is unabashedly proud of the movies he did with Corman and other low-budget masters. "I'm probably more pleased about [them] than I should be," he told *Playboy*. "The beauty about most of these early films is that I was—for the most part—working with the same group of actors and writers who hung around the parties in coffee shops." Jack even got the opportunity to work on some screenplays: *Flight to Fury* and *Ride in the Whirlwind,* for example.

Nicholson had met and married his first (and, to date, only) wife, Sandra Knight, in 1962, after a blink-of-the-eye courtship, with Jack's closest buddy, actor Harry Dean Stanton, serving as best man. Jack was evidently and understandably smitten by Knight's considerable beauty, and soon after they wed, they worked together in *The Terror,* an unusually bad movie even by Corman's standards. The marriage would last six years and, in 1963, produced Jack's first child, Jennifer. As his life progressed, Jack may have thought he was ready to get married—he later told *Time* magazine that he felt "secret inner pressure about monogamy"—but he wasn't. He was getting more and more work and was becoming consumed by his career, and also: He never reined himself in from seeing other women on the side. He and Sandra parted company in 1968.

Looking back on it all from the perspective of stardom, Nicholson saw clearly that domestic life didn't stand much of a chance with him. Sandra wanted them to be a normal couple and all that, but Jack Nicholson as part of a normal couple . . . "My marriage broke up during the period when I was acting in a film during the day and writing a film at night," he said later. "I simply didn't have time to ask for peace and quiet or to say, 'Well, now, wait a second, maybe you're being unreasonable.' I didn't have the twenty minutes I felt the conversation needed. . . . I've blown a lot of significant relationships in my life because I was working and didn't have time to deal with a major crisis."

He and Sandra would stay on good terms in the years after the divorce. "Our marriage was lived out rather than failed," he said. "We just grew apart. We were so obviously going in different directions that we were becoming a burden not only to each other but to the child."

Professional promise, personal trial. There was no predicting that Jack Nicholson's next chapter would be stardom.

Jack's first big-budget movie experience was in *Ensign Pulver* (1964), Josh Logan's tepid follow-up to the much more successful *Mister Roberts*. The movie was a critical and commercial flop, but the experience introduced Jack to several of the up-and-coming young actors of the era, including Larry Hagman—Jack introduced him to marijuana—James Farentino, Robert Walker Jr., James Coco and Peter Marshall. The one shadow over this otherwise sunny scene: June, whom Jack still believed was his sister, succumbed to cancer just a short time after shooting began in Mexico.

AMERICAN INTERNATIONAL PICTURES/PHOTOFEST

Terrible Terror Not all of Corman's productions were of the cringingly bad variety. Given a decent budget and more experienced actors, he occasionally collaborated on more substantial fare like *The Raven* (1963), in which Jack shared the screen with three legends of the horror genre: Peter Lorre (above), Vincent Price and Boris Karloff. Faced with such an array of impressive talent, all of whom were eminently capable of mining the campy spoof for laughs, Jack chose to play it absolutely straight, giving a winningly deadpan performance.

Such brief brushes with quality never prevented Corman from continuing to grind out the B-movie dreck. After wrapping *Raven* and with two days left on his rental of the castle set and on his contract with Karloff (opposite, above)—Price and Lorre were gone—Corman decided to produce another horror film called *The Terror,* whose only claim to fame may be that it featured Jack and his wife, Sandra Knight, (opposite, below), who shared several excruciating scenes with her husband. The movie was shot as much as possible in the remaining two days, then finished in the ensuing months, whenever Corman found the cash and the work-for-nothing actors to help him. *The Terror* was truly terrible—more horrible than horror. Ten years later, then an established star, Jack would say, "*The Terror* embarrasses me as much as anything."

COLUMBIA PICTURES presents the **monkees**

and Victor Mature! and Sonny Liston! and Annette Funicello! and Carol Doda!

in "a fun-movie that encompasses every other movie form—western, desert saga, war film, musical, horror film, science fiction! It's memorable!"

"head"

"A movie for a turned-on audience!"

Monkee Business   One of Jack's stranger film forays was his pivotal role as the writer and co-producer of *Head* (1968), which teamed him for the first time with director and close friend Bob Rafelson. Nicholson and Rafelson would go on to collaborate on many movies, most notably *Five Easy Pieces*, but *Head* cannot be counted among their triumphs. Hoping to capitalize on the success of the Beatles' two movies (*A Hard Day's Night* and *Help!*), the film is an almost bewildering pastiche of unrelated skits, dialogue, and visual tricks, all intended to capture a youthful, psychedelic-crazed audience, only this time the focus was not the Fab Four from Liverpool, but rather the Monkees (from left, with Jack, Davy Jones, Michael Nesmith, Micky Dolenz and Peter Tork), the pop group created and marketed by Rafelson. Monkees mania peaked during the first two seasons of their television show, but by the time of the movie's release in 1968, the craze was definitely on the wane. In spite of cameos from the likes of Dennis Hopper, Annette Funicello, Frank Zappa, Victor Mature and Sonny Liston, the movie lasted only four days in theaters.

CHAPTER THREE

A Ticket to Ride

*His journey to stardom was hardly without a
bump or two, but once Jack jumped
on the bike with Peter Fonda in Easy Rider,
his destination was never in doubt*

*I*N THE RICH annals of Hollywood there have been few runs of greatness to match the one on which Jack was about to embark—though it all began rather inauspiciously.

Is inauspiciously right? Let's say weirdly, in the way that everything in the later 1960s seemed to be happening weirdly—and the American cinema in particular was changing in weird and often wonderful ways.

In 1968, soon after making the low-budget *Hells Angels on Wheels*, Nicholson was approached about appearing in another biker flick. Rip Torn, who was slated for the role, had gotten in a fight with the director, Dennis Hopper, so the part had come available. So, on the surface, another biker flick. But this film would turn out to be slightly different, and Nicholson sensed this early. As he read the script, he could see clearly that the production aspired to something more than B-movie drive-in filler. The casting was ambitious. Peter Fonda and Hopper himself, the latter of whom had worked with Jack on *Head*, were being pegged as emerging stars, if decidedly unconventional ones. Torn had been lined up for the part of George Hanson, an addled attorney for the ACLU, and that casting too indicated ambition, even if it didn't work out. With Torn out, Nicholson was in, and the rest would be, as they say, history.

Easy Rider is one of those films that isn't so much great as it is memorable, more intriguing artifact than towering work of art. Loopy and not entirely coherent—as said, it was directed by Hopper—it follows the exploits of two zonked-out drug dealers, Hopper and Fonda, as they gun their bikes from Los Angeles to Florida, searching for the soul of America. Or something like that. Along the way they get busted and find themselves in need of a lawyer. Enter Hanson, and his bottle.

As for substance abuse, during the making of the movie, Nicholson, Hopper and Fonda's overarching goal seemed to be to smoke as much dope as possible. The haze of pot that followed the three stars as they went about their work has become the stuff of Hollywood legend. By one account, the three of them did 155 joints while filming the famous campfire scene—a total that Jack protested was slightly exaggerated.

Arriving in theaters at the height of the Vietnam War—a year after the assassinations of Martin Luther King Jr. and Bobby Kennedy—the film hit a nerve. While Fonda's Captain America biker and the general counter-cultural milieu of the film was the focus, discerning critics noted that some real acting was going on in the margins. Nicholson's performance as the liberal lawyer was riveting, earning him his first Oscar nomination, this one for Best Supporting Actor.

And just like that, it seemed, Jack Nicholson could do no wrong. There followed *Five Easy Pieces* (1970), followed by *Carnal Knowledge* (1971), followed by *The Last Detail* (1973), followed by *Chinatown* (1974), followed by *One Flew Over the Cuckoo's Nest* (1975), which got him his first Oscar, for Best Actor. All in the space of slightly more than five years: Each of the films, in its way, a classic, and at least one of them, *Chinatown*, an indisputable masterpiece. Nicholson's performances were brilliant throughout.

From the very beginning of his career, and regardless of whatever intoxicants he might be ingesting, Jack always worked exceptionally hard at his craft. For *Five Easy Pieces*, in order to bring a strong measure of verisimilitude to the character of Bobby Dupea, who was once a classical pianist, he worked with teacher Josef Pacholczyk to perfect his fingering technique.

ARTHUR SCHATZ

We pause to emphasize here a couple of the collaborations noted in the photo captions of our book. At the end of his apprenticeship phase, he had hooked up with Bob Rafelson, another young and literate cineaste, on, of all things, the movie *Head*, starring the Monkees (that ersatz but quite fun band's TV show was Rafelson's first big break). Nicholson, as we have seen in the pictures, was an integral part of that very odd production; he had worked on the screenplay and even arranged some of the music. In this later, "serious" period, Rafelson was Jack's director on *Five Easy Pieces*, which is what really got Nicholson noticed by the intelligentsia, and which first forwarded his ability to personify danger (the diner scene) as well as bonhomie. And then there was Roman Polanski, director of *Chinatown*. He became a friend, and Nicholson supported him as a good friend might after Polanski's wife, the actress Sharon Tate, was murdered by the Manson family. Later, though, the statutory rape conviction that resulted in Polanski's flight and continued exile from the United States, and the derailment of whatever Hollywood career he might have enjoyed, stemmed from an incident at his friend Jack's house—Jack was out of town at the time. As well, Nicholson himself found that, suddenly privileged, he didn't always handle his new status well. His tricky temper, of which he had long been aware, began to flare in public as well as in private. After a long time in waiting, he either still wasn't ready for stardom, or was resentful that it hadn't come sooner.

Later, Jack would chuckle about the impression that he had been an overnight success, pointing out that he had made 20 movies before *Easy Rider*. "There were two ways up the ladder—hand over hand or scratching and clawing," he said. "It's sure been tough on my nails." He admitted he didn't deal with stardom with the aplomb he would have liked: "I was rude to friends—didn't return phone calls as promptly as I should. I never used to be late; suddenly I was late everywhere."

The filming of *Five Easy Pieces*, which is the very epitome of a career- and actor-defining picture, was interesting, to say the very least—with an upshot that attached too perfectly to his own hard-to-pin-down heritage. In contrast to the goofy but idealistic George Hanson of *Easy Rider*, here he was Bobby Eroica Dupea, a tortured former concert pianist who is both charming and volatile, a seducer who is also filled with self-loathing. During filming, Nicholson began a relationship with co-star Susan Anspach, which in short order produced a son, Caleb. But—and this is a big but—Jack said later that Anspach didn't tell him he was the father until six or seven years after the fact. In talking about it, Jack, a veteran of strange domestic battlefields, sounded more resigned than bitter. "I've never been allowed a real avenue to find out about [the true parentage]," he told *Rolling Stone* in 1984, when Caleb was thirteen. "She's an avant-garde feminist who—when I met her—was proud of the fact that she already had a child whose father no one knew." Eventually Jack and Caleb became close, though the animosity between Nicholson and Anspach would linger.

After *Five Easy Pieces*, Nicholson was on to *Carnal Knowledge*, where he gave a stunning

Nicholson was in classic Jack mode at the Academy Awards in 1976 after winning his first Best Actor Oscar for *One Flew Over the Cuckoo's Nest*. Director Milos Forman said this of his talented star: "You don't direct Jack, any more than you tell Wayne Gretzky where to hit the puck. You just make sure the two of you understand what it's about and you let him go."

interpretation of an even less sympathetic character. This time it was Jonathan, a tax attorney who, when he isn't processing returns, is auditing the sexual charms of every woman he comes across. "When I played *Carnal Knowledge*, I knew that women weren't going to like me for a while," he told *The New York Times* in 1986. "That was a given. I'm going to play the devil, and I don't want to play him safely. I want people to think Jack Nicholson is the devil. I want them to be worried."

Casting him in the lead of *Chinatown* was a bit of a risk for director Polanski. There are actors who seem to be so much a part of their time that it's hard to imagine them in any other era. With his insouciant smirk, ubiquitous onscreen in an era marked by insouciant smirks everywhere, Jack fell into that category. And yet, portraying private eye Jake Gittes as he makes his way around 1930s L.A., Nicholson, sticking closely to the script written by his pal Robert Towne, with whom he had shared an apartment when they were both starting out, pulled it off. Gittes was a smoothie, yes, but also a smug cynic, a would-be badass who's about to learn a lesson in just how terrifying the true badasses of the world can be. His character is tough, vulnerable and bewildered. *Five Easy Pieces* changed our thinking about Nicholson, and *Chinatown* changed it again.

An interesting side note: Nicholson has had the opportunity to utter some of the most famous lines in movie history, snippets of dialogue that have become cultural touchstones. There was his wild entry in *The Shining* to the cry of "Here's Johnny!" and the electrifying "You can't handle the truth!" speech from *A Few Good Men*. His insouciant and somewhat salacious suggestion of what can be done with the chicken salad sandwich in *Five Easy Pieces*. It's worth asking whether we remember them because of the words or the actor. "Here's looking at you, kid." Is it the same without Bogie?

"Sometimes," he has said, "when you read a script, you can tell when you reach the writer's favorite line. They are my least favorite lines because of the expectations." In other words: Give me some room to work my own magic. As a matter of fact, he added, it has become an obligation of his, once he has become famous, to avoid scenes that seek to score cheap points off his more familiar flourishes. "Much of my job . . . is to un-Jack the parts," he said. "When I read a script, I look for when they want me to be Jack-be-wild or Jack-be-nimble or Jack-be-whatever."

After *Cuckoo's Nest*, there was *Terms of Endearment* (1983), which won him another Oscar, for Best Supporting Actor, for what at the time seemed a very un-Jack role. Then followed *Prizzi's Honor* (1985), *Heartburn* (1986) and *The Witches of Eastwick* (1987).

Do you remember *Ironweed*, released in 1987, the adaptation of William Kennedy's great novel in which Nicholson played an alcoholic drifter opposite Meryl Streep? Nicholson remembers it. "*Ironwood* to me is one of the best movies I've done, but was it a commercial success?" he said. "Some movies are jazz, some are rock 'n' roll."

He has long been willing to perform all kinds of music.

By the time this photograph was taken in 1978, Jack had become one of the hottest commodities in Hollywood, with five Academy Award nominations and one win to his name, and a collection of directors and producers desperately wanting to cast him in their movies. Over the next decade his bankability would only increase.

PHOTO 12/POLARIS

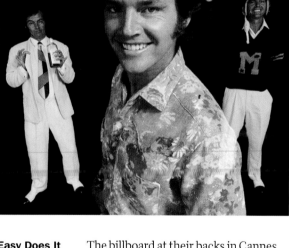

ARTHUR SCHATZ

SILVER SCREEN COLLECTION/GETTY

Easy Does It   The billboard at their backs in Cannes trumpeted Peter Fonda (top, far left) and Dennis Hopper (top, middle) as the leads of *Easy Rider* (1969), but the shooting star who emerged from the hit that caught the angst of a generation was Jack (top, right), who would receive the first of his many Academy Award nominations for his performance as George Hanson, the alienated, alcoholic small-town lawyer who joins Fonda (far right) and Hopper for a portion of their epic cross-country trip.

(The publicity shot at left, below, shows Jack as Hanson in the background, and in the foreground as Robert Dupea in *Five Easy Pieces*, though the smile is not characteristic of Dupea at all.) Jack's involvement in the project — Rip Torn was originally supposed to take the role, but an angry argument with the volatile Hopper opened the door for Jack — was in part as a peacemaker and all-around zookeeper for producers Bert Schneider and Bob Rafelson, who were deeply concerned about Hopper's well-established

reputation for erratic behavior. In fact, Hopper was stoned pretty much throughout the shooting and ended up producing an original cut of over 10 hours, then a director's cut of over four, which required several skilled editors, including Jack, to pare it down to the 95-minute film that finally was released. In addition to Jack, the other real star of the movie was cinematographer Laszlo Kovacs, whose breathtaking imagery of the American landscape elevated the road picture to the status of myth. Despite its mixed

reviews, *Easy Rider* was an instant hit when it opened in the U.S. in July 1969, with mostly youthful crowds lined up for blocks to see the movie in urban theaters around the country. And, as he knew from the moment he viewed the first rushes, Jack was catapulted to the status of major star. "Right about the time of *Easy Rider*," Jack said, "I had gotten myself locked right in to the sociological curl—like a surf rider—and found I could stay right in there, ride this, and cut back against it."

ARTHUR SCHATZ (3)

Father Jack Jack's marriage to Sandra—the only time he would ever walk down the aisle—ended for good with a divorce decree dated August 8, 1968, almost a year before his breakout performance in *Easy Rider* would hit movie screens around the United States. Both he and Sandra described the parting as amicable and indeed the pair would remain friends, though Sandra was awarded sole custody of their daughter, Jennifer (at home with Jack in 1969 on these pages and overleaf), and would soon move to Hawaii, thereby considerably limiting Jack's contact with his daughter during her childhood. Nonetheless, he faithfully stayed in touch, paid alimony and child support, and saw Jennifer as much as circumstances allowed, often inviting her to visit him on set. (She would later recall how overwhelmed she was by the beauty of Faye Dunaway during a visit to the *Chinatown* set in 1974.)

Longtime Friend In September 1969, soon after his breakout performance as burned-out small-town lawyer George Hanson in *Easy Rider*, LIFE sent photographer Arthur Shatz to Jack's new home on Mulholland Drive to capture the 32-year-old actor on the edge of stardom. In addition to pictures with his daughter, Jennifer (see previous four pages), the shoot included several candid moments with Jack and Bob Rafelson (above, with LIFE reporter Judy Fayard), soon to direct Jack in his next movie, *Five Easy Pieces*. Their association (and friendship) would span many years and would include Rafelson's involvement as producer or director on an array of Jack's films, including *Head, Easy Rider, Five Easy Pieces, The King of Marvin Gardens* and *The Postman Always Rings Twice*.

At Home and on the Road   From the time he bought it in 1969, Jack's house on Mulholland Drive, next door to Marlon Brando and down the street from Warren Beatty—an unholy trio if ever there was one—became the base of operations for Jack's legendary partying, though it's hard to believe that much of it took place in Jack's homey and surprisingly floral-dominated kitchen (above). During the 1970s, he could often be spotted buzzing around Los Angeles in his beloved Volkswagen (opposite). As he told LIFE reporter Judy Fayard, "Anyone out here who doesn't drive a Volks is either ostentatious or stupid." Fayard noted that Jack's outfit in these pictures represented "his standard driving regalia: peaked cap, Grand Prix medallion and yellow shades."

All the Pieces Fit   Jack's close relationship with Bob Rafelson (above), whose company produced *Easy Rider*, yielded another career highlight—and another Oscar nomination—the following year with Rafelson's direction of Jack in *Five Easy Pieces* (1970). Playing the alienated Bobby Dupea, Nicholson (opposite, with costars Karen Black and Billy Bush) willingly took on a complex and often negative character, in the process offering audiences one of the most compelling antiheroes in cinematic history. (Who can forget the famous chicken salad diner scene?)

Writing years later, film critic Roger Ebert would observe:

"It is difficult to explain today how much Bobby Dupea meant to the film's first audiences. I was at the New York Film Festival for the premiere of *Five Easy Pieces*, and I remember the explosive laughter, the deep silences, the stunned attention as the final shot seemed to continue forever, and then the ovation.

"We'd had a revelation. This was the direction American movies should take: Into idiosyncratic characters, into dialogue with an ear for the vulgar and the literate, into a plot free to surprise us about the characters, into an existential ending not required to be happy. . . . It was, you could say, the first Sundance film."

In the Driver's Seat   With the clout acquired from a pair of Oscar-nominated performances in *Easy Rider* and *Five Easy Pieces*, Jack was able to make *Drive, He Said* (1971), the movie he'd been interested in making since reading Jeremy Larner's novel of the same name in 1967. It would be Jack's first directing gig, and the result, while interesting in places, was a critical and commercial flop. Ultimately, Jack found the director's job truly torturous, though he did enjoy his role as the arbiter of casting, as evidenced in these pictures, taken as part of a LIFE story that chronicled his development

of the film. Here, Jack is auditioning actresses for the role of an exhibitionist cheerleader, a part that called for nudity and hence offered Jack the opportunity to request a parade of aspiring starlets to remove their clothes, not to mention perform a variety of gymnastic—and revealing—moves. It's good to be king.

SUNSHINE/ZUMA

Making a Masterpiece   Jack had always been known as a peacemaker on the set, but even his diplomatic skills could not quell the conflict between the autocratic but brilliant director Roman Polanski (above, with Jack, nose bandaged after being brutally slit by Polanski's character in the film), and the temperamental but brilliant actress Faye Dunaway (opposite), during the filming of *Chinatown* (1974), the masterpiece scripted by Robert Towne. In the end, the trio had collaborated on a classic, even though Polanski was uncomfortable about returning to the Los Angeles area, where his pregnant wife, Sharon Tate, had been murdered by Charles Manson's followers in 1969. The film, and the set, were fraught with Freudian undertones, as John Huston (right), the father of Anjelica Huston, whom Jack had just begun seeing, played monstrous patriarch Noah

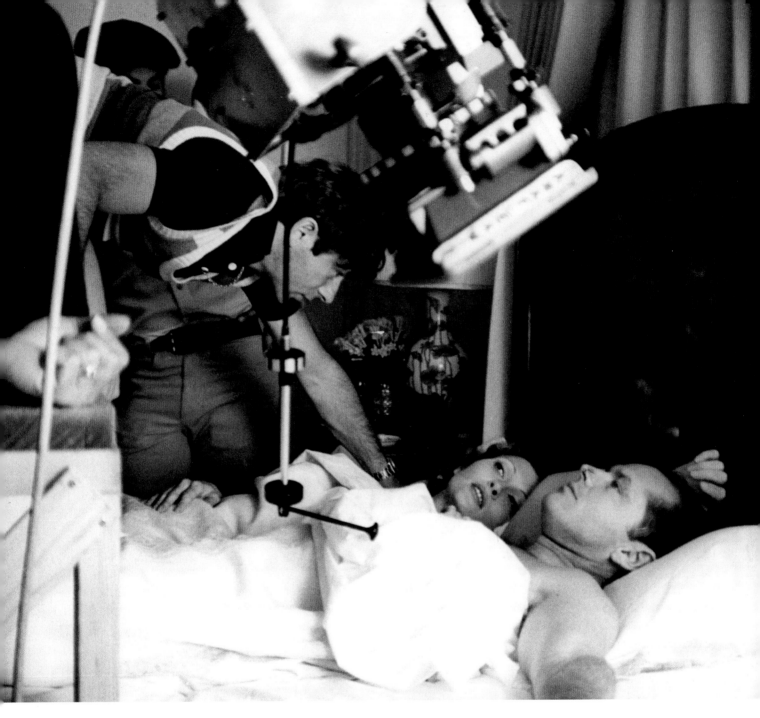

Cross, eventually revealed to be the rapist of his daughter, played by Dunaway. Polanski got his revenge on Dunaway by killing her character off at the conclusion of the movie, over Towne's strenuous objections. The film, replete with political as well as such personal complications—the central plot involves municipal corruption associated with water in and around L.A.—would earn Oscar nominations for Nicholson, Dunaway and Polanski, as well as for the movie itself. The latest list of the American Film Institute's top 100 films of all time puts *Chinatown* at No. 21. (*One Flew Over the Cuckoo's Nest* and *Easy Rider* come in at Nos. 33 and 84, respectively.)

A Role for the Ages   For many of his fans, Jack's most powerful performance was as the charismatic Randle McMurphy in *One Flew Over the Cuckoo's Nest* (1975). The original Ken Kesey novel of the same name had been a classic of the burgeoning counterculture ever since the early 1960s, when Kirk Douglas bought the film rights while the book was still in galleys. Over time, as one studio after another declined to greenlight the project due to its dark, tortured story about a charismatic iconoclast battling the forces of repression in a mental institution, Douglas became too old for the role himself and turned the property over to his son, Michael, who had attained a measure of notoriety as the costar of television's *The Streets of San Francisco* with Karl Malden. The younger Douglas decided to avoid the studios altogether, find independent funding for the relatively low-budget ($4.4 million) film, recruit a major star (Jack) for the central character and bring in little-known Czech director Milos Forman to direct. The film was shot in a mental institution in Salem, Oregon, where Nicholson and the entire cast (including, above, from left, Vincent Schiavelli, Danny DeVito and Brad Dourif, as well

as Christopher Lloyd, seated to Jack's left) spent weeks before filming, interacting with the inmates and developing an authentic sense of their characters, an experience that the easy-going Forman—he was as laissez-faire as Polanski had been controlling—allowed the actors to use for the significant bits of the movie that were improvised. Jack himself brought his experience with the inmates, as well as all the turmoil in his personal life, including his very recent discovery about his true biological mother, to his portrayal of the funny, profane, complex, and ultimately heroic McMurphy, surely one of the most memorable characters in cinematic history. One of the film's real revelations was the performance of Will Sampson as the seemingly deaf and dumb Chief Bromden. Sampson had never acted before—he was an assistant warden at Mt. Rainier National Park—but his embrace of the lobotomized McMurphy (opposite) at the movie's climax is unforgettable. The film would sweep all five major Oscars, the first film to do so since *It Happened One Night* in 1935: Best Picture, Best Actor (Jack), Best Actress (Louise Fletcher, brilliant as the steely Nurse Ratched), Best Director (Forman) and Best Adapted Screenplay (Laurence Hauben and Bo Goldman).

JERRY WATSON/CAMERA PRESS/REDUX

GLOBE/ZUMA

JULIAN WASSER

Man About Town To say that during his Hollywood heyday Jack was a guy who got around would be an understatement. While increasingly unavailable to the media, except for the occasional and usually brief interviews to promote a movie—he has not gone on the talk show circuit since 1971—he nonetheless was often photographed at one event or another with an array of the Hollywood glitterati, such as (clockwise, from below) then-girlfriend Michelle Phillips and Mama Cass Elliot of The Mamas and the Papas; Warren Beatty (at a fundraiser for the legal defense of porn star Harry Reems, with mustache); Kirk Douglas and Beatty again, in 1977; Fred Astaire; and old friend Sally Kellerman in 1972. Jack claims that he got his signature style of wearing sunglasses everywhere, even indoors, from Astaire: "I was sitting next to Fred Astaire at the 1976 Oscars and we were having a few laughs. They announced his category and he didn't win and that minute he put on his sunglasses. I don't even think I had a thought, I just reached for the glasses. And that's why. I wear all kinds. I have too many sunglasses."

SAM EMERSON/POLARIS

NATE CUTLER/GLOBE/ZUMA

Everybody's Buddy

As the 1970s rolled on, Jack became a fixture on the Hollywood scene: Throw a party, hold a big event, stage a concert, and there was a pretty good chance Jack would be there. Clockwise, from above, he shares a moment with Bruce Springsteen (left) and fellow E Street Band member Steven Van Zandt (to Jack's right); with Michael Douglas, a pal since *Cuckoo's Nest* at Douglas's wedding in 1977; in a cab outside a Georgetown disco with Linda Ronstadt and Carl Bernstein, whom he would later portray in *Heartburn*; and at a party with Peter Falk and Michelle Phillips.

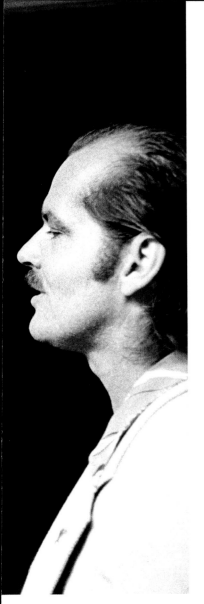

PARAMOUNT/KOBAL/ART RESOURCE, NY

UNITED ARTISTS/KOBAL/ART RESOURCE, NY

BURT GLINN/MAGNUM

Among Legends   Throughout his career, Jack always showed great respect for the show business legends who blazed the trail for his generation. One such elder was Groucho Marx (near left, with Jack, at a Democratic fundraiser in 1972), who hosted Jack at his home on several occasions. At one such luncheon in 1973—the other guests were Elliott Gould and Marcel Marceau—Groucho's grandson remembers Jack encouraging Groucho to accept an offer from the NBC warehouse in New Jersey to deliver the 16mm footage of Groucho's classic game show, *You Bet Your Life*, to his home. Resistant at first, Groucho eventually accepted the idea, and a classic piece of television history was saved from the trash heap. Director Elia Kazan (above) was another favorite of Jack's—he had watched Kazan's *On the Waterfront* over and over when it was released in 1954—but when Jack was up for the lead in *The Last Tycoon*, Kazan, over the objections of legendary Hollywood producer Sam Spiegel, strongly favored Robert De Niro for the part. In the end, De Niro got the starring role and Nicholson landed a supporting part. It would be Kazan's last picture and Nicholson's first and only with De Niro.

Working with an Idol Ever since he was a teenager, Jack had idolized Marlon Brando, thrilling along with the rest of the nation to Brando's riveting performances in *On the Waterfront* (1954) and *A Streetcar Named Desire* (1951) and imagining himself one day occupying a place of equal stature in the Hollywood firmament. When it came time to buy a house in 1969, he chose one next door to Brando on Mulholland Drive, and though Brando could be a touchy neighbor—he once called the police to complain about one of Nicholson's raucous Halloween parties— the two, while hardly friends in the early years, coexisted comfortably. When Jack got the chance to costar with Brando in *The Missouri Breaks* (1976), he jumped at the chance. In the three years since Brando's career resurrection in *The Godfather* and *Last Tango in Paris*, he had ballooned to 250 pounds and seemed to have

lost all taste for acting, preferring to focus on the cause of Native American rights—he refused to accept his *Godfather* Oscar, sending activist Sacheen Littlefeather to accept on his behalf and make a statement protesting Hollywood's treatment of Native Americans—as well as on the pursuit of women and fine food. Brando was less than generous to Nicholson during the filming of *The Missouri Breaks*, taking the eccentric character of bounty hunter Robert E. Lee Clayton and driving him over the edge into farce, even wearing a bonnet and Mother Hubbard dress in one scene. His quirky, downright weird performance overwhelmed the movie, which toppled under the weight of his eccentricity. Though frustrated, Jack never lost his reverence for Brando and the two became closer in the years that followed, sharing several investments and even buying neighboring condominiums in Bora Bora.

WARNER/MPTVIMAGES

Always Riveting

Jack's unforgettable star turn in *The Shining* (1980) as Jack Torrance, the blocked writer who descends into madness during a winter spent as the caretaker of the empty Hotel Overlook, came about in part because Jack thought the script, adapted by Diane Johnson from a Stephen King novel, was brilliant, but also because the film offered him the opportunity to work with much-admired director Stanley Kubrick. Kubrick was an unusual combination of perfectionist—he did literally dozens of takes of several key scenes—and laissez-faire actor's advocate, who advised Jack to view the script as a guide, from which he was free to depart or improvise when he felt it appropriate, as Jack did when crowing "Here's Johnny!" after his character wields an axe to break through a locked bathroom door (left) to get to his terrified wife, played by Shelley Duvall. "The film . . . belongs to Jack Nicholson," Kevin Thomas wrote in the *Los Angeles Times*. "No matter how you regard *The Shining* itself you're likely to be dazzled by Nicholson."

Jack took on the role of playwright Eugene O'Neill in *Reds* (1981) in large part as a favor to his old friend Warren Beatty (opposite, above, with Jack and Diane Keaton), who made his solo directorial debut with this sprawling epic about American John Reed's romantic obsession with the Russian Revolution. It was Jack's first portrayal of a historical figure and he researched the part extensively. "I hadn't done much biographical acting," he said. "And I really felt I got good brain contact there with Eugene O'Neill." His performance earned Jack his sixth Academy Award nomination.

Based on William Kennedy's Pulitzer Prize–winning novel, *Ironweed* (1987) represents one of the forgotten gems in Jack's astonishing collection of exceptional performances. Jack would say that his depiction of the alcoholic Francis Phelan was based on tales of his own broken, alcoholic grandfather, but whatever the inspiration, the performance was pure gold. Teamed for the second time with Meryl Streep (opposite, below), Jack clicked so well with his costar that both were nominated for Academy Awards. "Jack Nicholson commands the screen," David Ansen would write in *Newsweek*, "with the quiet weathered authority one associates with the great stars of the past—the Bogarts and the Tracys. His charisma isn't about glamor, it's about soul."

JERRY WATSON/CAMERA PRESS/REDUX

Family Matters   Another year, another great performance for Jack, this time in *Terms of Endearment* (1983) as the washed-up, womanizing former astronaut Garrett Breedlove, who wins over the reluctant, starchy Aurora Greenway, played by an equally brilliant Shirley MacLaine, enjoying a lighter moment with Jack at left. The film marked a turning point for Jack as he came to accept, and even embrace, the ravages of age, perhaps even exaggerating them a bit as he does in the classic bedroom scene when he removes his robe to reveal a big-time middle-aged paunch. "I just swelled it out to make it look as big as possible," Jack said. "My baby elephant look, I call it." The banter between Garrett and Aurora offered abundant laughs in the midst of an otherwise tragic story and confirmed the Nicholson-MacLaine combination as one of Hollywood's most endearing. The role would win Jack his second Oscar, this time as Best Supporting Actor.

Prizzi's Honor (1985), which cast Jack as a wise-guy hitman in love with another mob assassin played by Kathleen Turner (right, with Jack in gangster garb), struck just the right

comic note, charming audiences and providing a showcase for his on-again off-again girlfriend Anjelica Huston—she and Jack slept in separate rooms at the Carlyle Hotel during filming in New York—as well as for director John Huston (above, left, with Anjelica and Jack), her father and a surrogate father to Jack. Both men were nominated for Oscars, but Anjelica, at 34 and only then coming into her own as an actress, was the only one to come away with the coveted statuette. John and Jack were both in tears as she accepted the award.

JOHN BRYSON

ZADE ROSENTHAL/PARAMOUNT/KOBAL/ART RESOURCE, NY

CHAPTER FOUR

The Joker

*Stardom for Jack meant a cavalcade
of earthly pleasures, including parties, drugs
and a parade of beautiful women*

*I*T TELLS YOU much that you need to know about this aspect of his life that Jack Nicholson once felt compelled to correct any misimpressions by asserting, "I've never been in an orgy of more than three people." Good for you, Jack. That's probity at the turn of the millennium. Good for you.

Hollywood history is chock full of bad boys, everyone from Errol Flynn to Robert Downey Jr., and even slyly not-really-bad boys like George Clooney, who nudge and wink and know that we know that they know. Jack, regularly alongside Warren Beatty, his fellow conspirator in the last decades of the last century, straddled the actual and the joke. When it came to eyebrow raising conduct—drugs and sex and such—he very much enjoyed his excesses. And he knew that we knew that he knew that we knew. He didn't mind a bit.

Jack, a Willie Nelson among actors, started smoking pot almost as soon as he arrived in Hollywood and admitted that he had used grass frequently since around 1960. Yes, this might have been appropriate for his character in *Easy Rider,* but even that was problematic. Consider: At the beginning of the campfire scene, he, Hopper and Fonda are supposed to be straight. "So after that first take or two, the acting job becomes reversed," he said. "Instead of being straight and having to act stoned at the end, I'm now stoned at the beginning and have to act straight and then gradually let myself return to where I was—which was very stoned." A pro's pro.

Cannabis was hardly the only illicit substance to be found on the *Easy Rider* set. While filming near Taos, New Mexico, Nicholson and Hopper dropped acid while visiting the nearby tomb of author D.H. Lawrence. This was not Nicholson's first encounter with LSD, not hardly. He told *Playboy* that he had started with that stimulant in the early 1960s—one of the first people in this country, he maintained, to try it. "You think it's going to be like getting stoned on grass," he said. "But all of your conceptual reality gets jerked away and there are things in your mind that have in no way been suggested to you: such as you're going to see God; or watch sap streaming through the leaves of trees; or you're going to feel the dissolving of certain bodily parts; you're going to re-experience your own birth, which I did on my first acid trip."

His preferred intoxicant, along with marijuana, has always been women. Kim Basinger, his costar in *Batman,* called him "the most highly sexed individual I've ever met." As we've already seen, his wandering eye contributed to his breakup with Sandra Knight. Since then, he has shared his bed with an untold number of women; asked once if it was true, as reported somewhere, that he had slept with 2,000 women, he testily replied, "Hell, I don't count."

For more than thirty years, his main base of bachelor and all other operations has been his sprawling mountaintop compound on Mulholland Drive. For a good chunk of time, his two neighbors were fellow fellows Marlon Brando and Warren Beatty. As in, yikes! It is in a secluded locale, and this suits Nicolson. "I've had days in my life, or three or four days at a time, or weeks, when I've been with more than four women," he has said, while adding that he isn't proud of the fact: "I found that to be an internal lie. You're just not really getting it on past a certain point. It's unrealistic—like going for some endurance record. Everybody knows that's a pure ego trip."

Nicholson's lifelong ego exercise has included

While Jack's reputation as a womanizer was certainly fully justified, he also has had a cadre of close, long time women friends who never became sexual conquests, including actresses Sally Kellerman and Carol Kane, and screenwriter Carole Eastman.

strange doings—of course it has, everyone knows that. Some extremes are too much fun to ignore in a career recounting. For a time there in the 1960s, he became a full-fledged nudist. There you go! For three months or so, he didn't wear a stitch of clothing while in the house, even when receiving visitors. For him, it was perhaps liberating or maybe another form of acting—a chance to experience reality in a different way. "Once I decide to do something, I don't do it partially," he said, "so when I did this, I was nude no matter who came by." The reaction of his guests during this period varied. The actor friend Harry Dean Stanton loved it. On the other hand, his old pal Roger Corman, hardly someone whom anyone might call uptight, "didn't like it much." Nor, as might be expected, did Nicholson's daughter, Jennifer, who was just a young child at the time. But Nicholson found it an interesting experience while it lasted: one more thing he would enjoy for a time, but choose not to pursue indefinitely.

If Nicholson has been a habitual womanizer—and he has been—he has also enjoyed several serious relationships, associations with women who mattered more. A number of them have been high-profile achievers in the movie business. We have discussed Susan Anspach. Another early period Hollywood romance was with Michelle Phillips, of The Mamas and the Papas fame, with whom he started keeping company in 1971. At the time, Phillips was coming off an eight-day marriage to and divorce from Nicholson's buddy Dennis Hopper. "I started taking her out because she was depressed," Nicholson explained. Being a gentleman, he was sensitive to Michelle's feelings; being a mate, he had, of course, cleared all this with Hopper ahead of time. "As my feelings

for Michelle deepened," he said, "I told her up front, '[L]ook, I don't want to constantly define the progress of this relationship. Let's keep it instantaneous.'" Whatever that might mean. It is surely unsurprising that Jack Nicholson has issued some of the most interesting pickup lines in the history of Tinseltown.

The spontaneity kept the relationship with Phillips fresh, and it lasted close to three years. Jack insists that, contrary to commonly held assumptions, it is usually the woman who leaves him. He concedes that his behavior may leave them no other choice, but still: for the record. He notes as well that he considers it important to maintain a good relationship with his exes, and by and large, he does.

By far his longest steady relationship was with Anjelica Houston, which lasted seventeen years. They started dating around the time Nicholson was making *Chinatown,* which costarred Anjelica's father, John Huston. Anjelica was 22 years old, 14 years younger than Nicholson. The relationship was long but stormy, with Anjelica angered by Jack's repeated infidelities and Jack having to deal with her retaliatory actions, such as a dalliance with his good friend Ryan O'Neal, an episode that put him in an unaccustomed position. "I didn't blame her in the beginning," he said, "I think being my girlfriend has so many things even I couldn't deal with that I can honestly say I don't blame her, although I was hurt. But—it doesn't make you feel better."

For years, Jack danced around the question of marrying Anjelica. "I'm iconoclastic about marriage," he said 11 years into his relationship with her. "I got married at one time not thinking one way or the other about it. I just did it. I didn't

Jack's bachelor pad on Mulholland Drive remains his primary home to this day and while he has added to it—he bought Marlon Brando's neighboring property after Brando's death in 2004 and tore down Brando's decaying home—he remains most comfortable nestled away in privacy in his original retreat overlooking Franklin Canyon.

feel threatened. I loved the girl, but it wasn't a big time act to me. Just like not being married now isn't." The hesitance was probably just as well, considering the events that transpired. For one thing, while involved with Anjelica, Jack fathered another child, by Danish model Winnie Hollman. This daughter, named Honey, was born of an affair that Nicholson managed to keep secret from Anjelica—at the time. More problematic—at the time—was the waitress/model Rebecca Broussard, who was pregnant in 1989, while Jack was still with Anjelica. She knew about this one right off the bat, and it proved to be the last straw. She was so furious that she burst into Jack's office at Paramount and began to beat him with her fists. "Yeah," I probably deserved it," Jack told *Vanity Fair*. The bruises were not just physical. When he talks about the pain of that breakup he sounds entirely sincere: "The reality was that I was annihilated emotionally by the separation from Anjelica, That was probably the toughest period in my life."

The breakup was followed by an even stormier romance with Broussard, who was the same age as Jack's daughter Jennifer (with whom she was also good friends). There was an electricity to the relationship, perhaps, but was it a teen-agey electricity? "The first time Jack Nicholson touched my hand, I almost blacked out," Broussard once said. "I saw flashes of light." The lights would dim, but before they did, their union produced two children, Lorraine and Raymond. Jack wasn't sanguine about any long-term prospects, as he told *Rolling Stone* in 1998: "She's a pyrotechnical personality. She disagrees with me a lot, and, you know, at some moments I'm not loving it."

That same year, Nicholson began keeping company with Lara Flynn Boyle, an established young actress, with the accent on *young*: 33 years his junior. As Boyle memorably remarked, "The whole country has a love affair with Jack. Why can't I?" Why, indeed—everyone's entitled!—and that dalliance lasted around two years.

For all his hell-raising, Jack has, mostly, kept his nose clean—at least compared to other super celebrities' noses. No drug busts or drunk driving incidents splashed in the tabloids. He does, admittedly, have a bit of a temper—actually, more than a bit. He was driving in North Hollywood in 1994 when, he later said, another motorist cut him off. Both vehicles stopped at the light. Jack emerged from his, brandishing a golf club, which he then used to smash the windshield of the other driver's Mercedes. He was charged with vandalism and assault. Jack claimed the guy had tried to run him over. The case was eventually settled out of court. In an interview 10 years after the fact, he was still dismissing the kerfuffle as much ado about nothing: "That was a lapse. I didn't think I would do any harm. It was a graphite golf club. I thought it would shatter."

When he wasn't golfing in this period, he was making movies and building his filmic (as opposed to Page Six) legend. He was the Joker in Tim Burton's *Batman*; he won more Oscars; he issued those indelible lines. He became "Jack." Courtside at the Lakers games or front row at the Oscars were bereft spaces without Jack. But they would never be bereft, because Jack was always there, shades in place, but the shades hiding not a thing, rather embellishing all. If it were suggested to Jack that he was a true piece of work, he might answer, "Yeah."

Director Burton admired Jack's creative approach to the role of the zany Joker. "He can come up with different approaches to a scene time after time," Burton said, "and I'd find myself wanting to do extra takes just to see what he would do."

JULIAN WASSER

Life With Anjelica   Although they never married, it is fair to describe Jack's relationship with Anjelica
Huston as the most serious and enduring of his life. The daughter of famed actor
and Hollywood director John Huston, Anjelica nonetheless spent most of her childhood in Ireland and
Europe before a brief stint as a model in New York City, where she met Jack at one of artist Andy Warhol's
parties. So she was a novice in Hollywood when she and Jack began seeing each other in 1973—he was
36 and she was 22—and Jack helped introduce her to the sometimes bewildering world of the movie
business. In the beginning, the couple was inseparable, whether at home (above, and opposite, above),
or at big events like the Academy Awards (opposite, below, in 1976, with Jack's daughter Jennifer, when
Jack won his first Oscar for *Cuckoo's Nest*). Anjelica and Jennifer were close, and for the first time since
his marriage to Sandra in the 1960s, Jack enjoyed a measure of domestic stability. But soon, Jack's
womanizing and partying took their toll, and when Jack conceived a child with the much younger
Rebecca Broussard in 1989—Anjelica herself had very much wanted a child with Jack—that proved to be
the last straw and the couple split, some 17 years after their first meeting. "I was devastated by our having
to separate," she said, "but there was no choice." In spite of their sometimes tortured history, the pair has
remained friends and mutual admirers ever since.

Vivid Villainy Jack was always a shrewd judge of talent, and he was immediately drawn to up-and-coming director and iconoclast Tim Burton, whose macabre imagination was on ample display in his successful hits, *Pee-wee's Big Adventure* (1985) and *Beetlejuice* (1988). So when Nicholson was offered a role in Burton's *Batman* (1989), as the Caped Crusader's nemesis, the Joker, he was interested. Fully aware of Jack's star power as well as the critical importance of the villain to the comic-book genre, Warner Brothers agreed to Jack's request for one of the more lucrative contracts in history: $6 million up front and an astonishing 10% (reports vary) of the gross and licensing fees. With the movie eventually raking in $425 million worldwide, it is estimated that Jack's take on the picture was $60 million. The movie's opening was a national event, as audiences flocked to see Burton's vision of a brooding Batman, played by Michael Keaton, and a dark, uneasy Gotham City, brought to jarring, electric, frenzied life every time Jack appeared onscreen as the lunatic Joker. Now past his milestone 50th birthday, Jack (left, with costar Kim Basinger) proved himself yet again willing to do whatever it took to bring a role to life and excite an audience. As the 1980s came to a close, Jack was still the brightest star in the Hollywood firmament. In a poll of leading critics conducted by *American Film* magazine, he was named the actor of the decade, narrowly edging out Robert De Niro.

One Big Happy Family

In 1996, Jack experienced one of those classic Hollywood rites of passage, the inclusion of a star in his honor on the Hollywood Walk of Fame. Rebecca Broussard (far right) attended the festivities with Jack and their children, Raymond (on her lap) and Lorraine (next to Jack), along with Jack's eldest daughter, Jennifer, and her daughter—Jack's first grandchild—Sean. Jack and Rebecca were still together, though living separately, and infidelities on both sides would soon erode the relationship beyond repair.

Jack, in signature shades, is front and
center as usual at the 2013 Academy Awards

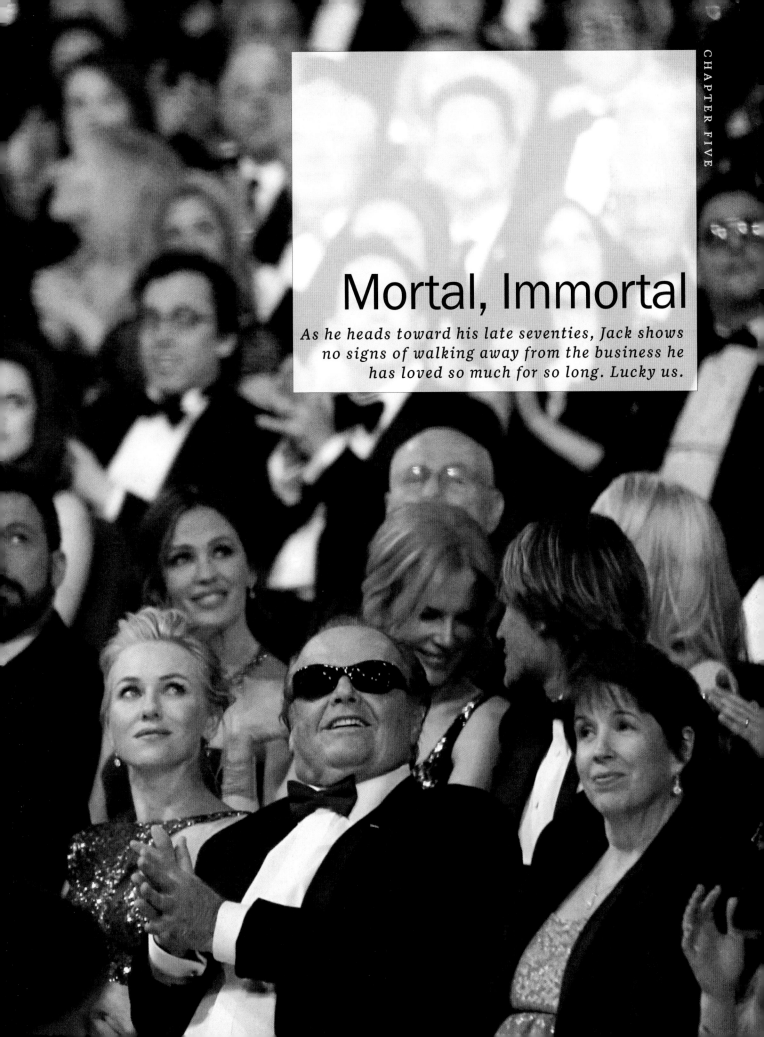

CHAPTER FIVE

Mortal, Immortal

As he heads toward his late seventies, Jack shows no signs of walking away from the business he has loved so much for so long. Lucky us.

EVEN IN 1968, he was older— older than Fonda, older than the kids buying tickets. He was an older service guy in *The Last Detail,* and senior to many of the other inmates in *One Flew Over the Cuckoo's Nest.* As the Joker, he was an eminence, cashing a big check, to be sure, but also gracing—blessing—a youth-targeted megafilm with his considerable presence (his buddy Brando had played Superman's father, after all). In *A Few Good Men* and *Terms of Endearment,* he was a receding-hairline superstar showing how it's done. In later career, he has exacted his due with not-bad fare like *The Bucket List*—hey, De Niro, Hoffman and Streisand did the Focker movies—but if he were to turn an astonishing trick tomorrow, in another Scorcese or a Shakespeare, no one would any longer be surprised. Long ago, he became Jack Nicholson and he remains Jack Nicholson, the man of surprises. There are no longer questions with this guy. He will astonish us regularly, and he will regularly turn up where we expect to find him. His seat ringside at the Oscars as much as his seat courtside with the Lakers is reserved, and if he's missing, for any reason, it will be noted. That would be a surprise.

He swings the golf club now, and not just at other people's cars; he took up the game at age 52. He still skis at age 76 and in winter departs Los Angeles for snowy Aspen. Unless, of course, there's a game on—a Lakers game; that is his adult drug: "It's the most competitive thing on the planet. That's what I like." He means this seriously. He has said about one of the Lakers' arch-nemeses, the Boston Celtics' Larry Bird: "Bird's like me. . . . Somebody said about him that Bird doesn't come to play, he comes to win."

Certainly, winning is something that Jack knows. He has all the hardware, and he's rich as Croesus. "I've been good to the movie business, and, sure, it's been good for me," he said. "That's why they call people like me 'the money.' I've always been uncomfortable with it, but it's the way it is. 'Where's the money?' I am the money."

He remains a very interesting guy. By one appraisal, roughly $100 million of his $400 million net worth is tied up in artwork that he has collected over the years. Visitors have marveled at the Picassos and Chagalls and Matisses that adorn the walls of his Mulholland Drive home. And unlike some celebrity collectors, who use art as just another status symbol, Jack actually has a deep appreciation of what he's looking at. "I just like art. I get pure pleasure from it. I have a lot of wonderful paintings, and every time I look at them I see something different," he told *Parade* in 2007. "I never thought about paintings as money. I bought only one I could afford at the time."

As with most things in his life at this stage, the story is A-list: His encounter with the big-time art world came courtesy of Diana Vreeland, the legendary fashion doyenne, who took him to an auction in England in the early days. From then on, he couldn't get enough of it. In a memoir, Anjelica Huston's half-sister Allegra describes how Jack at one time kept a guest room always

While most often associated with the bright lights of Hollywood and L.A., Jack has always loved the wilds of Aspen as well, where he owned a home with record producer Lou Adler for 33 years until the pair sold the house for $11 million in 2013.

HARRY BENSON

at the ready for his old chum and costar from *Carnal Knowledge*, Art Garfunkel. It was available, that is, until Jack became, in effect, a truly high-end hoarder. "He collected paintings to the point of obsession," said Allegra. "Jack bought so many paintings that they soon overflowed the wall space and had to be stacked against the walls of the Garfunkel Suite, as the maid's room was known." There were eventually limits to even his zeal. "Everyone has their choking price," he said in 2008. "Recently, I was bidding in my bedroom, lying there, and once I went past $10 million, I started to feel the sweat come on all over." That was one game Jack lost . . . or maybe won: "In the end, it was a relief not to get it."

Inevitably, the years of cigarettes and late nights and heaven only knows what else have finally started to catch up with him. He says he doesn't go out much anymore and his face has taken on the look of someone who has seen perhaps a bit too much of what the world has to offer, good and bad. He says he's never really considered cosmetic procedures. "I haven't had surgery," he told *Vanity Fair*. "I don't want to be judgmental, but some of the things you see these days in Hollywood are a bit horrifying. . . . I'm not worried about wrinkles, on myself or a woman. I find them interesting."

Ah, yes, women: With Jack, sooner or later (and almost always sooner) it gets back to that subject. A certain wistfulness now comes over him as he contemplates the end of his swashbuckling days. "There were points in my life where I felt oddly irresistible to women," he told the *Daily Mail* in 2011. "I'm not in that state now and it makes me sad."

Jack Nicholson's charmed existence has always been disturbed by thoughts of death. (The existential dread would surely come naturally to someone who considers Camus one of his favorite authors.) "One of the toughest parts of aging is losing your friends," he said in 2011. "At first it starts quietly, then pretty soon it's every month, and you can't help but think, 'When is that bell going to go off for me?' and on top of that you feel this consistent loss. At this time of life, you feel just a sword's point from death. It's frightening—who wants to face God and the clear white light? I know I definitely don't. Yet."

The answer, as it has always been for him, is to keep working. He has spoken vaguely of retirement from time to time, but no one seriously thinks he will ever stop making movies. All the anxiety and effort that come with mastering a new part are a tonic for him. He looks like an old blues guitarist; he seems destined to die in harness.

So these days he takes delight in his children, his art, his cigars—and lets it go at that. As for us, his audience, we're left with a remarkable body of work—films and performances that will be watched and savored for generations to come—and whatever he might do next. In lesser hands, the jaded, slightly decadent personality might have curdled into something unappealing. Instead, Jack Nicholson molded it, with a kind of stoicism (not a word often applied to him) that has built to a scruffy greatness. "I like that line I wrote, that we used in *The Border*, where I said, 'I just want to do something good before I die'," he once said. "Isn't that what we all want?"

Intimations of mortality surround Jack at every turn as he finds the funerals mounting by the year. At left, he presents an unusually pensive mien while attending the funeral of Senator Edward Kennedy in 2009.

A Trio of Gems   Jack lost a lot of weight in preparation for his four intense scenes—he earned $5 million up front and was required to be on the set for only 10 of the 68 days of shooting—in Rob Reiner's adaptation of Aaron Sorkin's play, *A Few Good Men* (1992). Surrounded by an array of recently minted stars, including headliner Tom Cruise, Kevin Bacon, Demi Moore and Kiefer Sutherland, Jack was intent on proving himself up to the challenge of the young guns. In the event, to no one's surprise, he more than held his own, ultimately uttering the line that still lives on in movie history, uttered during the climactic courtroom scene with Cruise: "You can't handle the truth!" As summed up by Peter Travers in *Rolling Stone*: "His presence electrifies the film. Nicholson is a marvel—fierce, funny and coiled to spring. Oscar is bound to salute." Indeed, Jack's performance earned him his 10th Academy Award nomination.

The five years after *A Few Good Men* were not particularly kind to Jack. His *annus horribilis* was 1994, which included this stunning litany of disasters: His half-sister, Pam Liddicoat, is murdered; his dear friend, producer Harold Schneider, drops dead of a heart attack; Jack is charged with attacking a man's car with a golf club in a fit of road rage; a cocktail waitress named Jennine Gourin tells the tabloids that she is carrying Jack's baby; and his turbulent relationship with the much younger Rebecca Broussard, while resulting in two beloved children, approaches meltdown. Into this somewhat bleak landscape rode Jack's pal, director James L. Brooks, who offered him another role just as juicy as Garrett Breedlove in *Terms of Endearment*, Brooks's blockbuster hit from 1983, which garnered Jack his second Oscar. This time, in *As Good as It Gets* (1997), Jack plays a very un-Nicholson type character in the obsessive-compulsive borderline agoraphobic Melvin Udall, whose nasty, mean-spirited assaults on everyone in his orbit keep the world at bay. A spirited but lonely waitress, played by Helen Hunt (top, right), comes to his rescue, the reclusive Udall is redeemed and even Jack's gay neighbor, played by Greg Kinnear, has a happy conclusion. For Jack, the ending was even happier, as the movie earned him his third Oscar and proved to the world that, after the lean years, Jack was back.

Jack returned to a role much closer to his traditional persona in *Something's Gotta Give* (2003) as aging Lothario Harry Sanborn, who finds his attentions drawn from his typically much younger girlfriends to the more age-appropriate Erica Barry, played with tremendous verve by Diane Keaton (above), who had seen little of Jack since 1981, when they had both appeared in *Reds*, but whom Jack still called by the nickname he bestowed on her so many years ago: Special K. Directed by Nancy Meyers, the picture really belonged to Keaton, but Jack brought his usual élan to his character, who ultimately gets the girl in spite of having to deal with a much younger competitor in the person of Keanu Reeves' character. Although opening in the Christmas 2003 season against the third and final installment of the *Lord of the Rings* trilogy, the movie was a huge hit, taking in over $100 million by mid-January. No car chases, no special effects, no kids—could the old folks still draw a crowd?

RON FREHM/AP

Jokerman and the Joker   Jack has always adored Bob Dylan, so when he was offered the chance to present Dylan with a Lifetime Achievement Grammy in 1991, he jumped at the chance. Dylan was as inscrutable as ever—he has been even less forthcoming than Jack about personal details—giving an acceptance speech completely devoid of the typical list of names to be thanked, choosing instead to comment, "It's possible to be so defiled in this world that even your mother and father won't know you. But God will always believe in your ability to mend your ways."

FRÉDÉRIC RÉGLAIN/GAMMA-KEYSTONE/GETTY

GARY LEWIS/MPTVIMAGES

A Popular Guy   Jack is enormously beloved in France, so it was no surprise in 1990 when he received the Commander of Arts and Letters Ribbon from Culture Minister Jack Lang (above, with Jack and Rebecca Broussard). "The French public and I share a great fondness for you," Lang said in bestowing the award on a very pleased Jack, who had spent the summer in lovely Saint-Jean-Cap-Ferrat with Rebecca and their infant daughter, Lorraine.

The Golden Globes have been every bit as kind to Jack as the Oscars, and he was in classic Jack mode, with shades and cigar, at the 1998 event (left), where he received the Golden Globe as the best actor in a musical or comedy for his work in *As Good As It Gets* (see page 87). Two months later, the Academy Awards would follow suit, and any lingering doubts about Jack's enduring talent and popularity were entirely dispelled.

WARNER BROS/KOBAL/ART RESOURCE, NY

Leo, Martin and Jack

After three consecutive comic roles, Jack was looking for something darker when Leonardo DiCaprio began urging him to accept the role of mob boss Frank Costello in Martin Scorcese's newest picture, *The Departed* (2006). Jack agreed to join the stellar cast, which included Matt Damon and Mark Wahlberg, in addition to DiCaprio, but with one important condition: He wanted permission to improvise when he felt a scene called for it. Scorcese (middle, with Jack and cinematographer Michael Ballhaus) readily agreed. So emboldened, Jack gives a classic high-intensity, almost over-the-top performance, frequently surprising his fellow actors with vivid improvised moments — in one scene he unexpectedly pulls a gun on DiCaprio, in another he lights a table on fire — and, as so often in the past, the movie really comes to life when Jack is onscreen. To no one's surprise, given the talent involved, the movie is a hit, raking in more than $120 million in 2006. Critical acclaim comes at the Academy Awards: Scorcese is named Best Director; the movie wins Best Picture.

The Young and the Old of It   Jack was adamant about doing a better job with his two youngest children, Raymond and Lorraine (14 and 15, respectively, at the time this photo was taken at the 2006 Oscars), than he had with his other kids, and indeed pretty much from the time of their birth he transformed himself into a doting father, spending three hours a day, three days a week, at Lorraine's preschool, attending soccer games and other kids' events, renovating the guest house on his property for their use as they got older, hiring figure skating champion Tai Babilonia to work with Lorraine, buying their mother, Rebecca Broussard, a home in Bel Air, and sharing a passion for basketball with Raymond, who baited his Lakers-loving dad with his enthusiasm for Michael Jordan and the Chicago Bulls. Life had given Jack a final shot at parenthood, and this time he was going to do it right.

Morgan Freeman (far right) joined the cast of Rob Reiner's *Bucket List* (2007) first, playing Carter Chambers, a mechanic with cancer, who befriends billionaire and fellow cancer sufferer Edward Cole and persuades him to embark on a two-man quest to do all the things their lives had not allowed them to do. When Reiner approached him, Morgan had a request: "Rob said, 'I've got this great script, and I want to do it and I want to do it with you.' I said, 'All right.' I read it and said, 'In the right hands, this is going to be terrific.' So I called him up and said, 'It's nice but there's a caveat here: you need to get one actor.' And he said, 'who?' I said, 'Jack Nicholson.' So he said, 'Jack? All right, let's try it.'" Reiner, who had directed Jack in *A Few Good Men*, discovered that Jack wanted to work with Morgan as much as Morgan had wanted to work with Jack, and while the movie is a trifle, the chemistry between the two accomplished 70-year-old actors is worth the price of admission. When asked about his own late-in-life wishes, Freeman said, "This [working with Jack] has been on my bucket list for a long time." The pair proved, as Jack had already done many times, that Hollywood does not belong only to the young: The movie grossed a whopping $175 million worldwide.

CHRIS PIZZELLO/REUTERS

Sideline Star   Late in life, Jack's two abiding interests are his children and his beloved basketball. From his expensive courtside seat—first at The Forum, now at the new high-tech Staples Center—Jack can be spotted at virtually every home game, cheering the Lakers on or occasionally getting into the ear of the officials or a rival coach like Doc Rivers (shown above during the 2008 NBA Finals), the skipper of the Lakers' hated rivals, the Boston Celtics. On a particularly good night, like the one in 2005 when the picture at right was taken, all is truly right in Jack's world: the Lakers on the court and his daughter Lorraine at his side.

LUCY NICHOLSON/REUTERS

Shaquille O'Neal (opposite), the massive seven-foot-one center who led the Lakers to three consecutive NBA titles from 2000 to 2002, was a favorite of Jack's and the admiration was always mutual, so when Shaq's uniform was retired at halftime of a game against the Dallas Mavericks this past April, he wanted the team's most legendary fan to be a part of the festivities. "Jack's been sitting in that same seat for years, telling the referees, 'You can't handle the truth!' " O'Neal told the crowd, who responded with raucous applause.

Should we be surprised that, even at 75, Jack can still engender that kind of wildly enthusiastic response? Surely not. For all of us he's touched through the years, who have been moved to laugh or cry or cringe by one of his vivid performances, there will always be only one Jack. No last name needed.

Just One More

At 68, when this shot was taken during the filming of *The Departed* in 2005, Jack had mellowed a bit but still could kick up his heels. To this day, he retains an infectious enthusiasm that lifts the spirits of everyone associated with him: fellow actors, directors and, ultimately, of course, the audiences that flock to his films. Jack's last movie, *How Do You Know* (2010), was directed by James L. Brooks, who had provided Jack with wonderful vehicles in *Terms of Endearment* and *As Good As It Gets*, but this time Brooks misfired and the film was an expensive disaster. We eagerly await Jack's next performance, certain that his presence onscreen will electrify us as it always has. Here's to not just one, but many, many more.